TABLE OF CONTENTS

Up and Down the Aisles

Preparing a holiday meal requires organizational skills and planning.

Your family is getting ready for Thanksgiving dinner, and it's time to hit the grocery store to stock up on food. You need everything from turkey to turnips. Where do you begin? How can you make sure you are getting the best deals?

Your local grocery store or supermarket needs to sell its goods and keep its customers happy. This is how they survive as a business. There are several ways they do this. Some stores have employees greet you as you arrive. Others offer to carry your purchases to your family's car.

Grocery store employees make sure the shelves are stocked and that customers can find what they need.

Other methods of keeping customers and boosting sales are less obvious. Many store layouts guide you to certain products in a certain order. Store managers research different layouts to determine which ones lead to the highest sales. The more time you spend in a store, the more merchandise you will probably buy. Every item is arranged in a specific way for a specific reason.

REAL WORLD MATH CHALLENGE

Manuel's father asks him to go to the grocery store. He gives him $10.00 to buy a head of lettuce and some brown rice for tonight's dinner. He tells Manuel that he probably will need to use no more than half of the $10.00. Manuel arrives at the store at 4:00 P.M. and intends to leave by 4:15 P.M. He becomes sidetracked as he searches for the items he is supposed to buy. He leaves at 4:35 P.M. and has spent $8.00. He bought two additional products that he thinks will go well with dinner. **How much more time did Manuel spend at the store than he originally expected? How much more money did he spend than he planned to spend? What percentage of his father's money did he actually use?**

(Turn to page 29 for the answers)

Milk, eggs, and bread are often located at the back of the store. Fresh fruits and vegetables, breads, meats, cheeses, and frozen foods are found along the perimeters, or outside aisles. Inside aisles contain food that is packaged or canned. The end of most aisles features an endcap. This is a display of merchandise the store is promoting. It may involve special prices or bargains in an effort to get you to buy a certain product.

Fresh fruits and vegetables are usually found along one of the outside aisles of a grocery store.

Expensive goods are usually placed at eye level. Lower-priced products are frequently on one of the bottom shelves. Most people will buy what is in front of them rather than bend over to search areas that are less accessible. Some items are generally grouped together to promote sales. For example, tomato sauces are often found next to the pasta. Canned pie filling is usually near the flour and sugar.

Does all this make the grocery store seem like a giant maze? Don't get nervous—just think of the supermarket as a huge game board. You are the game piece. Your goal is to get through the checkout counter with the healthiest products you can find for the best possible prices. There are both obstacles and rewards along the way. Your math skills and your knowledge of nutrition are sure to help you win the game of grocery shopping!

CHAPTER TWO

GET FRESH!

Some grocery stores are small and sell fewer items.

As you walk into the store, you know you want to purchase foods that

are fresh and nutritious. But how can you tell whether one peach is better

than the next? Is a specific package of ground beef actually healthier than

Look for fruit that is firm and has no brown spots.

all the others? You need to pay attention when you are playing a game.

You also need to keep your eyes open and your senses alert when it comes

to picking groceries. A few simple clues can help make your shopping

experience quicker, healthier, and less complicated.

When selecting produce, choose fruit that is firm instead of mushy. A fresh piece of fruit should also have a light fragrance. Vegetables should be firm and crisp. Gently turn the produce over to make sure there are no brown or soft spots, but never pinch or squeeze it. This can cause fruits and vegetables to bruise or possibly even lose some of their juice.

There are several ways to evaluate meat, poultry, and fish. First, read the label on the packaging. The weight and price per pound should

Learning & Innovation Skills

How can you be sure that the fruits and vegetables you choose have a variety of nutrients? Experts say that people get the most nutrients by consuming a variety of fruits and vegetables that feature several different colors. So the next time you're at the grocery store, check out the produce department to see what your choices are. Then make it a point to fill your cart with produce from several of the following color categories:

- **White:** cauliflower, onions
- **Green:** broccoli, spinach, green beans, lettuce
- **Yellow:** yellow peppers, squash, bananas
- **Orange:** pumpkins, carrots, oranges
- **Red:** tomatoes, strawberries, red peppers
- **Purple:** grapes, plums
- **Blue:** blueberries

If you shop in a store with a fresh meat counter, you can ask the butcher for tips on buying the best meats.

be listed. You should also see a sell-by date. This gives you an idea of how fresh the meat, poultry, or fish is. If you do not plan to eat your purchase by the sell-by date, you should freeze it. Your best bet is to buy a package with a sell-by date that is still several days away. If you have any additional questions, a butcher frequently works behind a counter in this section of the store and may be able to assist you.

REAL WORLD MATH CHALLENGE

Bella is shopping on April 10. She purchases a package of chicken that weighs 2 pounds (0.9 kilogram) and costs $7.00. **How much does the chicken cost per pound?**

Bella isn't sure when she plans on cooking the chicken. Her mother doesn't like to leave fresh meat in the refrigerator for more than two days. **By what date should Bella place the chicken in the freezer?**

(Turn to page 29 for the answers)

Fresh produce, meat, poultry, and fish are typically your healthiest

options at the grocery store. But sometimes it's simply more convenient

and cost-effective to buy canned or frozen items. Luckily, many of the

same rules apply when evaluating both types of food. Most foods will have

an expiration date. This means the food must be consumed by that date.

Keep an eye out for dents in cans or any damage to packaging. This could

Nutrition Facts
Serving Size 1/6 package (60g)
Servings Per Container 6

Amount Per Serving		Mix	Prepared
Calories		260	360
Calories from Fat		80	150
	% Daily Value*		
Total Fat 9g*		14%	26%
Saturated Fat 3.5g		18%	30%
Cholesterol 0mg		0%	1%
Sodium 360mg		15%	20%
Total Carbohydrate 46g		15%	16%
Dietary Fiber 1g		4%	4%
Sugars 28g			

Food labels provide information about serving sizes, number of calories per serving, and other nutrition facts.

mean that the food is no longer healthy to eat. And don't forget to read the label. Reading labels and asking questions about nutrition are key parts of shopping.

REAL WORLD MATH CHALLENGE

Keisha is buying fruit at the grocery store. She knows that fruit only stays fresh for a short time. Different types of fruit vary in the number of days that they stay fresh. **Calculate the average number of days that each of the following fruits will stay fresh:**

Ripe peaches stay fresh for 3 to 5 days.

Ripe pears stay fresh for 7 to 10 days.

(Turn to page 29 for the answers)

CHAPTER THREE

DO THE MATH: WHAT TO BUY AND HOW MUCH TO GET

Comparing labels and selecting the healthiest foods is an important part of shopping.

As you stroll up and down the aisles, you see food items ranging from

chocolate bars to cucumbers to chicken nuggets. Sometimes you need

only one or two specific groceries. Other times you might be shopping

Each color on the food pyramid represents a food group. Visit www. mypyramid.gov for more information on food groups and healthy eating.

for meals for the entire week. You know it's important to make healthy

selections. What combinations of foods will provide the best source of

nutrition? Just as important, what serving sizes should you keep in mind

as you debate how much to buy?

Visit www.MyPyramid.gov to learn more about how to make the healthiest decisions at the supermarket. The food pyramid places foods in the following categories: grains, vegetables, fruits, milk, meat and beans, and oils.

Grains are foods made from wheat, rice, oats, barley, and other whole grains. Vegetables can be fresh, frozen, canned, or dried. Whole fruits or 100 percent fruit juice are a part of the fruit group. Milk and products made from milk, such as yogurt and cheese, are in the milk group. Foods in the meat and bean group include meat (beef and pork, for example), poultry, fish, nuts, eggs, and beans (including black, kidney, and navy beans). The oils category features liquid oils such as olive and canola oil, solid fats such as butter, and other foods high in fat content such as mayonnaise and salad dressings.

*A set of measuring cups can help you figure out
how much of a food to serve each person.*

The Web site also includes information on serving sizes and how

many servings you need from each food group every day. Be aware that an

average 9- to 13-year-old needs 5 to 6 ounces (142 to 170 grams) of grain,

2 to 2.5 cups of vegetables, 1.5 cups of fruit, 3 cups (710 milliliters) of

milk, 5 ounces (142 g) of meat, and 5 teaspoons (25 ml) of fat each day.

REAL WORLD MATH CHALLENGE

Darius's mother is at the grocery store. She is considering buying salmon fillets for her family. A single fillet weighs about 6 ounces (171 g). Darius likes to eat a little meat at both lunch and dinner. **If he has 1/2 of a fillet for lunch, how much should he eat at dinner to get the rest of his daily recommended serving of protein?** Remember, experts recommend 9- to 13-year olds get about 5 ounces (142 g) of meat every day. **What percentage of his daily serving of meat will Darius have at lunch if he eats 3 ounces (85 g) of salmon?**

(Turn to page 29 for the answers)

When analyzing the items in your cart and trying to determine

appropriate serving sizes, it often helps to think of common objects you

can easily visualize in your head. For example, 1 cup of potatoes, pasta,

or rice is about the size of a tennis ball. A 3-ounce (85-g) serving of meat

is about the size of a deck of cards. A medium piece of fruit or 1 cup of

*People who are active need to eat more calories
than those who don't get as much exercise.*

leafy green vegetables is about the size of a baseball. A 1.5-ounce (42.5-g)

serving of cheese is about the size of four stacked dice. And 1 teaspoon (5

ml) of oil is about the size of the tip of your thumb.

Serving size is particularly important when it comes to perishable items such as fresh produce, meat, poultry, and fish. It is best to buy only what you know your family will consume. Be sure your family will use up all the portions you buy.

Pay careful attention to labels that feature nutritional information. These details give you a better idea of the serving size for each product. Labels also list data related to calories and nutrients. Use your math skills to evaluate this information and decide which items are the best buys for your health. Do you have to choose between that box of chocolate doughnuts and some frozen fruit bars? If

21st Century Content

How many calories should you consume? Most 10- to 12-year-olds need about 2,000 calories a day. Someone involved in sports or who moves around a lot burns more calories than someone who is less physically active. What happens if you eat more calories than your body uses in a day? The extra energy will be stored as fat in your body. In other words, you will gain weight.

you read the labels and are keeping track of your calories, you'll probably

select the fruit bars for dessert.

Now you know how to pick the most nutritious choices at the

supermarket. You also want to be mindful of money. You're close to

winning the grocery store game. A few additional tips will help you make it

to the finish line. Keep your calculator handy!

REAL WORLD MATH CHALLENGE

Leila's favorite lunch is peanut butter on whole wheat bread. When she goes to the store one morning, she decides to look at the nutritional label on the jar. **If a serving size is 2 tablespoons (28 g), and there are 14 servings, how many tablespoons of peanut butter are in the jar? If there were 180 calories in a 2-tablespoon (28-g) serving, how many calories would be in a 3-tablespoon (43-g) serving? How many calories would be in a 4-tablespoon (57-g) serving?**

(Turn to page 29 for the answers)

CHAPTER FOUR

DO THE MATH:
EATING WELL ON A BUDGET

*Your math skills can help you get the most
for your money at the grocery store.*

Y ou know how to review nutrition labels. Let's review a few simple ways to keep an eye on prices. You will save money and still get the healthiest items.

Buy fruits and vegetables in

season. Strawberries in January can cost more than $3.00 per pound.

You may be able to pick your own summer strawberries for about $1.00 per pound!

You can often get fresh produce for good prices at farmer's markets.

REAL WORLD MATH CHALLENGE

Danny loves peaches and often buys them from his local grocery store. During the summer—when peaches are normally **harvested**—he notices that these fruits cost $2.50 per pound. In the winter, he observes that peaches are $3.25 per pound at the same store. **If Danny buys 2 pounds (0.9 kg) of peaches in July, how much less will he pay than if he buys 2 pounds (0.9 kg) of peaches in January?**

(Turn to page 29 for the answer)

Meat, fish, and some poultry can be expensive. The good news is that you only need a small serving of these items each day. Beans, eggs, and low-fat peanut butter are less-expensive choices that also fall into the meat and bean group.

A helpful financial tip is to divide your money just like the portions on your plate. Spend most of your money on fresh fruits, vegetables, and grains. It also is a smart idea to sit down with your family and come up with a grocery list before you leave for the store. This way, you're more

Manufacturers often offer coupons as a way to get people to buy more of their products. You can find coupons online, in local newspapers, and sometimes even on the back of receipts at the checkout register. Coupons entitle you to a discount on products. Just be sure to read the fine print, though. Some coupons have expiration dates or are only good at specific stores within a chain.

likely to buy foods everyone prefers and not become

as distracted by items that may seem appealing but

that you don't really need.

REAL WORLD MATH CHALLENGE

Anita has $25.00 to buy ingredients to make a healthy, well-balanced meal for her family, which includes five other people. She knows that she needs to have enough money to pay for the food as well as the 7 percent sales tax. **Will Anita be able to pay for the items on the following menu? How much money—if any—will she have left over?**

3 pounds (1.4 kg) of beef roast	$7.98
5 pounds (2.3 kg) of potatoes	$2.39
2 pounds (0.9 kg) of carrots	$2.78
1 pint (0.5 kg) of grape tomatoes	$1.49
12 wheat dinner rolls	$1.99
3 pints (1.5 kg) of strawberries	$2.99
1 gallon (3.8 liters) of low-fat milk	$2.99

How much did Anita spend on each person in her family for this meal?

(Turn to page 29 for the answers)

CHAPTER FIVE

SHOPPING LIKE A PRO

Taking the time to clip coupons can save you money at the grocery store and other shops.

The next time you go into a supermarket, you'll find yourself moving through the aisles more quickly. You are a confident shopper. You now have a better understanding of nutrition and your ability to spend money wisely. One or two final ideas may put you ahead of the game. Perhaps you've already made a list and clipped coupons ahead of time. Consider getting even more organized. Try to arrange your list according to the layout of the store. For example, group all the frozen foods together.

Finally, don't be embarrassed to ask plenty of questions. The store employees and manager are there to help you. They want you to have a pleasant shopping experience. If you can't find an item or think something was rung up the wrong way at the cash register, speak up. Remember—you are the customer. The supermarket depends on your business and wants you to keep coming back.

By following these tips and using your math skills and knowledge of nutrition, you can transform a trip to the grocery store from a complicated board game into an easy win. It's your move—what aisle will you hit first?

Real World Math Challenge Answers

Chapter One

Page 6

Since Manuel planned to leave the store at 4:15 P.M. but actually left at 4:35 P.M., he spent an additional 20 minutes there.

4:35 − 4:15 = 20 minutes

Manuel initially believed he would spend no more than 1/2 of the money his father gave him, so he didn't think the bill would come to more than $5.00.

$10.00 x ½ = $5.00

He spent $3.00 over that amount.

$8.00 − $5.00 = $3.00

By the end of the shopping trip, Manuel had spent 80 percent of his father's money.

$8.00 ÷ $10.00 = 0.8 = 80%

Chapter Two

Page 13

The chicken costs $3.50 per pound.

$7.00 ÷ 2 = $3.50

If Bella purchases the chicken on April 10, she should freeze it no later than April 12.

10 + 2 = 12

Page 14

Ripe peaches stay fresh an average of 4 days.

3 + 5 = 8

8 ÷ 2 = 4

Ripe pears stay fresh an average of 8.5 days.

7 + 10 = 17

17 ÷ 2 = 8.5

Chapter Three

Page 19

If Darius eats 1/2 the salmon fillet at lunch, he'll consume about 3 ounces (85 g) of meat.

½ x 6 = 3

This means that he should eat about 2 ounces (57 g) of meat at dinner.

5 ounces − 3 ounces = 2 ounces

Darius will have 60 percent of his daily serving of meat at lunch if he eats 3 ounces (85 g) of salmon.

3 ounces ÷ 5 ounces = 0.6 = 60%

Page 22

There are 28 tablespoons (399 g) of peanut butter in the jar.

2 tablespoons x 14 = 28 tablespoons

There are 270 calories in a 3-tablespoon (43-g) serving of peanut butter.

180 calories ÷ 2 tablespoons = 90 calories per tablespoon

90 calories x 3 tablespoons = 270 calories

There are 360 calories in a 4-tablespoon (57-g) serving of peanut butter.

90 calories x 4 tablespoons = 360 calories

Chapter Four

Page 25

If Danny buys 2 pounds of peaches in July, he will pay $5.00.

$2.50 x 2 = $5.00

If Danny buys 2 pounds of peaches in January, he will pay $6.50.

$3.25 x 2 = $6.50

He will spend $1.50 more for peaches in January than he will in July.

$6.50 − $5.00 = $1.50

Page 26

Anita will have to pay $22.61 for the cost of the items plus $1.58 in sales tax, for a total of $24.19.

$7.98 + $2.39 + $2.78 + $1.49 + $1.99 + $2.99 + $2.99 = $22.61

$22.61 x 0.07 = $1.58

$22.61 + $1.58 = $24.19

She will have 81 cents left over.

$25.00 − $24.19 = $0.81

Anita spent about $4.03 on each person for this meal.

$24.19 ÷ 6 = $4.03

GLOSSARY

calories (KAL-uh-reez) the measurement of the amount of energy available to your body in the food you eat

consuming (kuhn-SUM-ing) taking in

harvested (HAR-vest-uhd) gathered or collected

nutrients (NU-tree-uhnts) ingredients in food that provide nourishment

nutrition (new-TRISH-uhn) how a person's body takes in substances that contribute to its health and growth

perimeters (peh-RIH-muh-turz) boundaries or outer limits

perishable (PARE-ih-shuh-bull) likely to spoil quickly without proper storage or refrigeration

portions (POR-shuhnz) parts or shares of something

poultry (POHL-tree) birds that are raised for their meat and eggs; chickens, turkeys, ducks, and geese are poultry

produce (PRO-doos) fresh fruits or vegetables that are grown on a farm or in a garden

FOR MORE INFORMATION

Books

Brown, Angela McHaney. *Produce Manager.* Austin, TX: Raintree Steck-Vaughn, 2000.

Guthrie, Donna W., Joy N. Hulme, and Robyn Kline (illustrator). *Supermarket Math.* Brookfield, CT: Millbrook Press, 2000.

Web Sites

American Diabetes Association—Shopping
www.diabetes.org/for-parents-and-kids/diabetes-care/shopping.jsp
Helpful information about reading labels on packaged foods

U.S. Department of Agriculture—MyPyramid.gov
www.mypyramid.gov/
Detailed information on the food groups and healthy eating

INDEX

ABOUT THE AUTHOR

Cecilia Minden, PhD, is a literacy consultant and the author of many books for children. She is the former director of the Language and Literacy Program at Harvard Graduate School of Education in Cambridge, Massachusetts. She would like to thank fifth-grade math teacher Beth Rottinghaus for her help with the Real World Math Challenges. Cecilia lives with her family in North Carolina.

21st
Century
Skills Library

REAL WORLD MATH: HEALTH AND WELLNESS

GROCERY SHOPPING BY THE NUMBERS

Cecilia Minden

Cherry Lake Publishing
Ann Arbor, Michigan

Published in the United States of America by Cherry Lake Publishing
Ann Arbor, MI
www.cherrylakepublishing.com

Math Adviser: Tonya Walker, MA Boston University

Nutrition Adviser: Steven Abrams, MD, Professor of Pediatrics, Baylor College of
Medicine, Houston, Texas

Photo Credits: Page 15, © Karen Kasmauski/Corbis; page 16, Illustration courtesy
of U. S. Department of Agriculture

Library of Congress Cataloging-in-Publication Data
Minden, Cecilia.
 Grocery shopping by the numbers / by Cecilia Minden.
    p. cm.
 ISBN-13: 978-1-60279-006-3
 ISBN-10: 1-60279-006-X
 1. Grocery shopping—Juvenile literature. I. Title.
 TX356.M55 2008
 641.3'1—dc22   2007003890

*Cherry Lake Publishing would like to acknowledge the work of
The Partnership for 21st Century Skills.
Please visit* www.21stcenturyskills.org *for more information.*